Totally WACKY FACTS ABOUT PLANETS and STARS

EMMA CARLSON BERNE

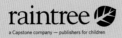

raintree
a Capstone company — publishers for children

THE UNIVERSE IS STILL GROWING – IT'S EXPANDING IN EVERY DIRECTION.

No one has worked out how big the UNIVERSE is.

The universe has no end, no edges and no boundaries.

Stars move at over 3.2 million kilometres (2 million miles) per hour as the universe EXPANDS.

MANY PEOPLE BELIEVE THAT THE UNIVERSE EXPLODED INTO EXISTENCE DURING THE BIG BANG.

Before the Big Bang, the entire universe was the size of a PEBBLE.

The universe expanded from a tiny mass in a TRILLION-TRILLIONTH OF A SECOND.

Before the Big Bang, there was NO SPACE and NO TIME.

You can still see the light from the Big Bang - it's called **COSMIC MICROWAVE RADIATION.**

cosmic microwave radiation as seen from a European Space Agency spacecraft

7

Your body is made up
of matter from
exploded stars in space.

Almost every atom in everything on Earth came from the BIG BANG or EXPLODED, DYING STARS.

SOME GALAXIES LOOK LIKE SPIRALS, SOME LIKE FLAT BALLS AND SOME HAVE NO PARTICULAR SHAPE.

You can see galaxies 2 million light-years away with the naked eye.

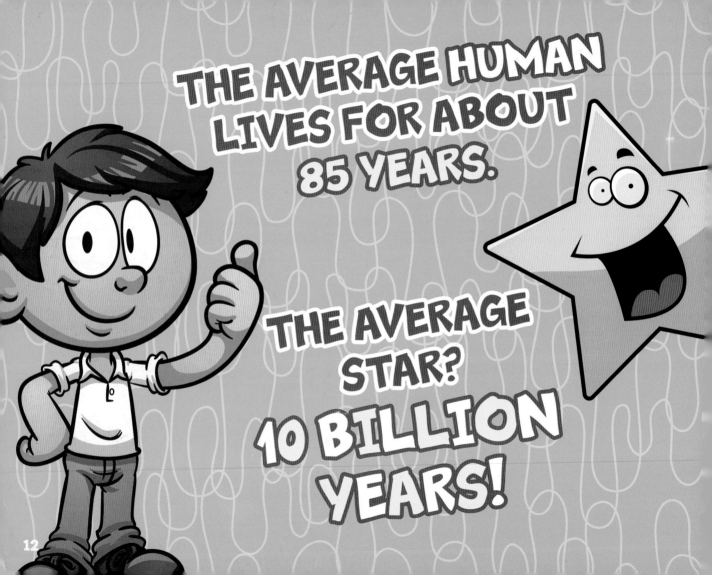

THE AVERAGE HUMAN LIVES FOR ABOUT 85 YEARS.

THE AVERAGE STAR? 10 BILLION YEARS!

EVERY STAR YOU SEE IS BIGGER THAN THE SUN. THE SUN LOOKS LARGER BECAUSE IT'S CLOSER TO EARTH.

The NORTH STAR rotates in a little circle every day.

THE PISTOL STAR, WHICH IS 25,000 LIGHT-YEARS FROM EARTH, IS AS BRIGHT AS 10 MILLION SUNS.

THERE ARE ABOUT A SEPTILLION STARS IN THE UNIVERSE – THAT'S 10 FOLLOWED BY 24 ZEROS!

When a huge star collapses, a **BLACK HOLE** is created.

The gravity inside a **black hole** is so strong, even **LIGHT** can't escape from it.

IF YOU WERE IN A BLACK HOLE, YOUR BODY WOULD STRETCH OUT LIKE A LONG PIECE OF SPAGHETTI.

Supernovas are giant explosions from the death of GIANT STARS.

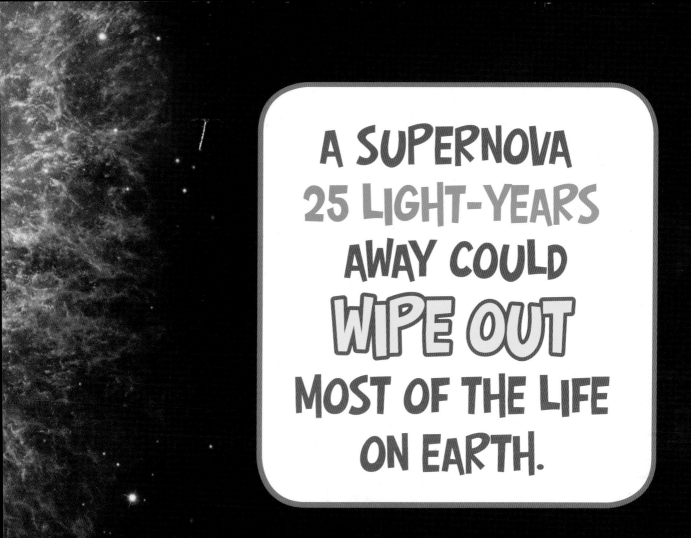

WHEN A SUPERNOVA EXPLODES, IT CAN OUTSHINE AN ENTIRE GALAXY.

In the Milky Way, supernova explosions happen about once every 50 YEARS.

In 1006 the **brightest star** explosion was recorded. It was so bright, even at midnight, people could have **read by its light.**

You can see light from star explosions that happened hundreds of years ago.

If our solar system were the size of a 10P PIECE,

the Milky Way would be the size of NORTH AMERICA.

THE MILKY WAY IS PACKED WITH ABOUT 100 BILLION STARS.

The **biggest star** in the Milky Way is 1,500 times bigger than the SUN.

The Sun makes as much energy as 91 billion tonnes of dynamite exploding EVERY SECOND!

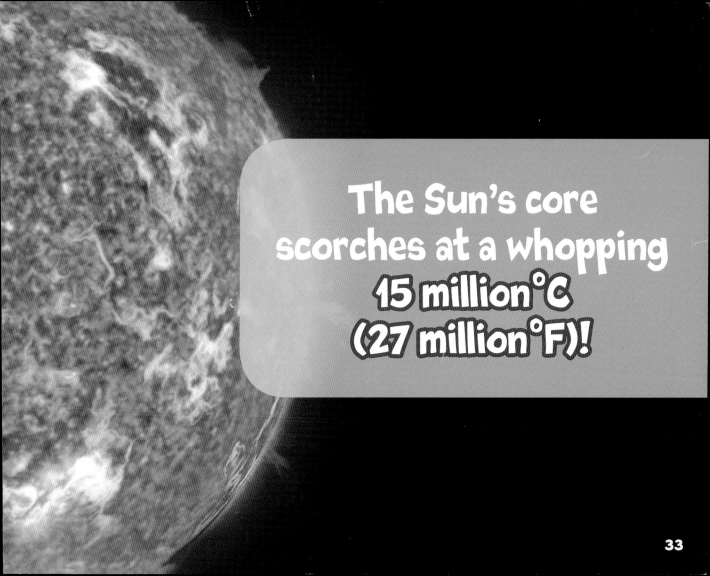

The Sun's core scorches at a whopping 15 million°C (27 million°F)!

An aeroplane from Earth would take 26 years to reach the Sun!

Sunlight takes three minutes to reach Mercury, but more than five hours to reach Pluto.

← Sun

Mercury

Pluto

The surface of the Sun burps and boils like a pan of **PORRIDGE.**

SOLAR FLARES SHOOT THOUSANDS OF KILOMETRES INTO SPACE.

If the Sun were the size of a **BASKETBALL**, Earth would be the **HEAD OF A PIN.**

LIFE ON EARTH WOULDN'T EXIST IF THE SUN WERE ANY **LARGER** OR **SMALLER.**

WHEN THE SUN
FINALLY DIES,
IT WILL BE
CRUSHED DOWN
TO THE
SIZE OF EARTH.

AS THE SUN GETS OLDER, IT GETS HOTTER.

The Sun's "fuel tank" is about half full – it has burned through about

E **HALF** F

its lifespan.

41

A 45-kilogram (100-pound) person would weigh more than 1,225 kilograms (2,700 pounds) on the Sun.

The Sun's GRAVITY keeps Earth from floating off into space.

DURING A LUNAR ECLIPSE, THE MOON TURNS A COPPER COLOUR.

Daylight looks like **TWILIGHT** during a solar eclipse.

The longest total solar eclipse lasted more than **7 minutes.**

The temperature on Earth can plunge **11°C (20°F)** during a total solar eclipse.

Every year, there are **two** solar eclipses somewhere on Earth.

LONG AGO SOME PEOPLE IN CHINA BELIEVED THAT A DOG BITING THE MOON HAD CAUSED A LUNAR ECLIPSE.

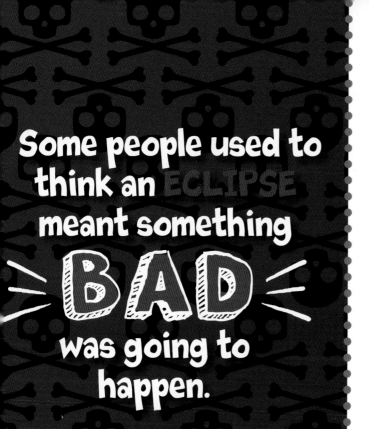

Some people used to think an ECLIPSE meant something **BAD** was going to happen.

ANCIENT INCANS BELIEVED THAT A LUNAR ECLIPSE WAS CAUSED BY A JAGUAR ATTACKING THE MOON.

THE MOON? I'd rather track down that deer!

49

Scientists recently found a planet that drifts by itself in space, rather than orbiting a sun.

A REQUIREMENT TO BE A PLANET? YOU HAVE TO BE ALMOST COMPLETELY ROUND.

There are eight planets that orbit the Sun:

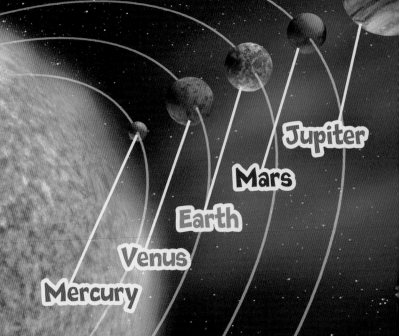

Jupiter

Mars

Earth

Venus

Mercury

52

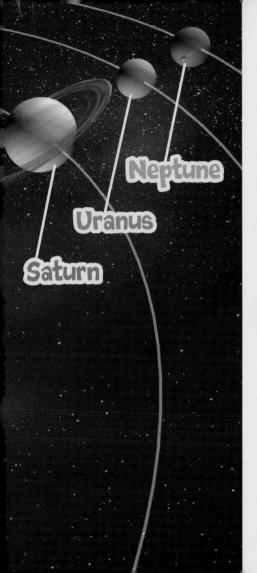

Saturn

Uranus

Neptune

YOU CAN SEE ALL OF THE PLANETS, EXCEPT NEPTUNE, IN THE NIGHT SKY WITHOUT USING A TELESCOPE.

Mercury's temperature can change 605°C (1,090°F) between night and day.

THE TEMPERATURE ON VENUS IS HOT ENOUGH TO MELT LEAD.

MERCURY HAS NO WIND, WATER OR ATMOSPHERE, WHICH MEANS IT ALSO HAS NO WEATHER.

From Mercury, the Sun looks three times larger than it does from Earth.

Even though it's closest to the Sun, Mercury is not the hottest planet.

From some parts of Mercury, the Sun appears to get larger as it rises, and to shrink as it sets.

The stars move across the sky **THREE TIMES FASTER** on Mercury than on Earth.

SOME CLIFFS ON MERCURY ARE 1.6 KILOMETRES (1 MILE) HIGH.

Mercury's surface looks similar to the Moon's.

ONE CRATER ON MERCURY IS MORE THAN 1,200 KILOMETRES (800 MILES) LONG!

Look carefully! You can see Venus in the sky during the DAY.

Venus is called Earth's sister planet – they are almost the SAME SIZE.

243 Earth days=
1 day on Venus

WHEN COMPARED TO THE OTHER PLANETS, VENUS ROTATES BACKWARDS.

"SNOW" ON VENUS IS MADE OF METAL.

Venus may have been full of water once, but it has all now BOILED AWAY.

It rains ACID on Venus.

THERE IS ALMOST NO LIGHT ON VENUS BECAUSE **THICK CLOUDS** COVER ITS ATMOSPHERE.

On VENUS the air pressure is so heavy, it would **CRUSH** a human.

EARTH ROTATES EVERY 23 HOURS, 56 MINUTES AND 4 SECONDS – NOT EVERY 24 HOURS.

EARTH'S ROTATION HAS SLOWED DOWN 1.4 THOUSANDTHS OF A SECOND IN THE LAST 100 YEARS.

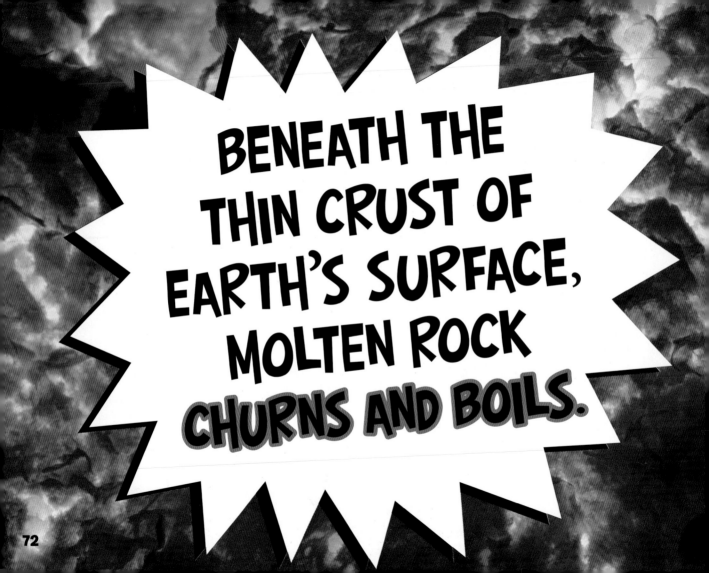

The temperature of Earth's inner iron core is 5,000 – 7,000° C (9,000 – 13,000° F)!

What's your FULL address?

Main Road, England,
Earth, the Solar System,
Orion Arm, the Milky Way,
the Local Group, the Virgo Supercluster,
THE UNIVERSE

Don't forget a stamp!

THE THINNEST PART OF EARTH'S CORE - THE CRUST - CONTAINS ALL THE KNOWN LIFE IN THE UNIVERSE.

MOST OF MARS IS RED-COLOURED, BUT THERE ARE PATCHES OF GREEN SOIL. SCIENTISTS DON'T KNOW WHY.

The soil on Mars is RED because it's full of RUST.

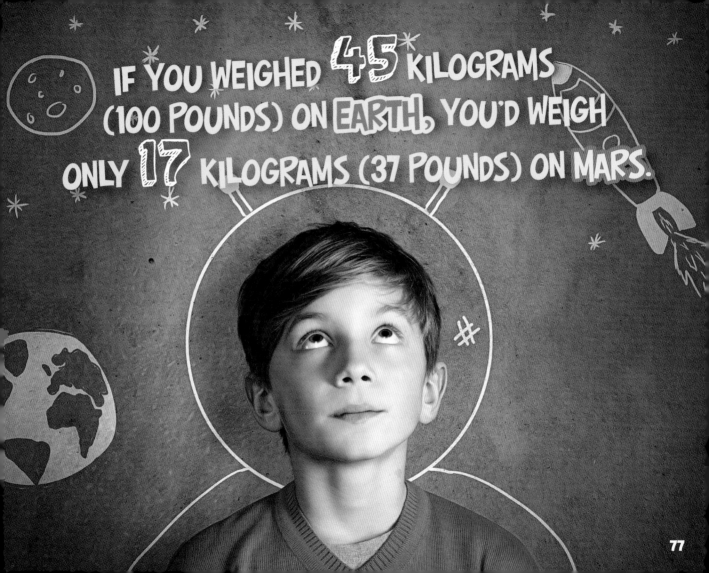

IF YOU WEIGHED 45 KILOGRAMS (100 POUNDS) ON EARTH, YOU'D WEIGH ONLY 17 KILOGRAMS (37 POUNDS) ON MARS.

The tallest mountain on Mars is two and a half times taller than Earth's

MOUNT EVEREST.

A HOT, ROCKY DESERT CALLED DEATH VALLEY IS THE CLOSEST ENVIRONMENT ON EARTH TO THAT OF MARS.

Mars has **SEASONS**, but they last **TWICE AS LONG** as the seasons on Earth.

IF YOU SPILLED WATER ON THE SURFACE OF MARS, IT WOULD **FREEZE** AND BOIL AWAY AT THE SAME TIME!

Jupiter's mass is two and a half times larger than that of all the other planets in the solar system COMBINED!

JUPITER IS CALLED THE "GAS GIANT".

JUPITER ROTATES SO FAST THAT THE PLANET SLIGHTLY FLATTENS.

Jupiter's day is only 9 hours and 55 minutes long!

ONE YEAR ON JUPITER EQUALS 11.8 YEARS ON EARTH.

Jupiter's oceans are made up of liquid hydrogen.

HUMANS COULD NEVER LIVE ON JUPITER BECAUSE IT IS COVERED IN CLOUDS OF

POISONOUS GAS.

JUPITER'S AIR PRESSURE

is so strong it can crush metal as if it is

CARDBOARD.

JUPITER HAS A LARGE SPOT CALLED "THE GREAT RED SPOT".

Humans have observed the Great Red Spot from Earth since at least **1831**, but possibly since **1665!**

The Great Red Spot is a gigantic, swirling storm that is larger than Earth.

THE GREAT RED SPOT IS SHRINKING.

Saturn rotates once every 10 hours and 34 minutes.

ITS FAST ROTATION MAKES SATURN THE FLATTEST PLANET.

The clouds on Saturn are made of poisonous **AMMONIA ICE CRYSTALS.**

Saturn's windstorms reach 1,600 kilometres (1,000 miles) per hour – twice as fast as an aeroplane.

THE RINGS ON SATURN ARE MADE OF CHUNKS OF ICE AND ROCK.

Saturn's rings are 300,000 kilometres (186,000 miles) long, but only 0.8 kilometres (½ mile) thick.

The chunks of ice in Saturn's rings can be as small as a grain of sand or as big as a house.

Uranus is so far away from Earth, it would take about 9 YEARS to get there in a spacecraft!

URANUS IS CALLED THE "ICE GIANT" BECAUSE IT'S MADE UP OF ICE AND ROCK.

Saturn isn't the only planet with rings - Uranus has them too!

Uranus was the first planet to be discovered with a TELESCOPE.

Uranus may have been hit by two **MASSIVE OBJECTS,** tilting the planet on its side.

BECAUSE OF ITS TILT, URANUS ROLLS LIKE A BARREL ON ITS SIDE.

Uranus takes 84 Earth years to go around the Sun once.

NEPTUNE IS MADE UP OF LAYERS OF GAS BUT HAS A CORE OF ROCK.

One year on Neptune is nearly 165 years on Earth.

BRRR!
THE AVERAGE TEMPERATURE ON NEPTUNE IS -225°C (-373°F).

WINDS WHIP

AROUND ON NEPTUNE AT NEARLY **2,000 KILOMETRES (1,200 MILES) PER HOUR.**

Scientists think there might be an ocean of **liquid diamond** on the surface of Neptune.

The dwarf planet Pluto was considered a planet until 2006.

Pluto is so cold that the air there can freeze and fall like snow.

DWARF PLANETS ARE SMALLER THAN EARTH'S MOON.

WONDERING HOW ALL OF

From smallest to largest, the planets are:
Mercury, Mars, Venus,
Earth, Neptune, Uranus,
Saturn and Jupiter.

THESE PLANETS COMPARE?

GLOSSARY

atmosphere layer of gases that surrounds some planets, dwarf planets and moons

Big Bang sudden event that many scientists believe caused the beginning of the universe

black hole invisible region of space with a strong gravitational field

eclipse when one object in space blocks light and keeps it from shining on another object in space

galaxy large group of stars and planets

gravity force that pulls objects together

hydrogen colourless gas that is lighter than air and burns easily

lunar relating to a moon

mass body of matter with no particular shape

Milky Way galaxy in which our Sun is located

molten melted by heat; lava is molten rock

orbit travel around an object in space; an orbit is also the path an object follows while circling an object in space

solar relating to the Sun

solar flare gas that shoots out from the Sun's surface

supernova exploding star

READ MORE

Mercury and Venus (Astronaut Travel Guides), Isabel Thomas (Raintree, 2013)

My Tourist Guide to the Solar System... and Beyond, Dr Lewis Dartnell (Dorling Kindersley, 2012)

Stars and Planets, Royal Observatory Greenwich (Collins, 2013)

WEBSITES

www.bbc.co.uk/science/space
Discover facts about the planets, the solar system and other astronomy topics.

www.esa.int/esaKIDSen/
The European Space Agency website for kids has fun facts, quizzes and games to help you learn more about the planets and stars in our universe!

INDEX

Big Bang 4–7, 9

black holes 22–23

cosmic microwave
  radiation 7

Death Valley 80

dwarf planets
  106–107

Earth 9, 15, 25,
  34, 38, 39, 40,
  43, 47, 57, 59,
  63, 64, 70–75,
  77, 78, 81, 87,
  90, 91, 98, 101,
  103, 106, 108

galaxies 10–11,
  26

Great Red Spot
  90–91

Jupiter 84–91,
  108

lunar eclipse 44,
  48–49

Mars 76–83, 108

Mercury 35, 54,
  56–61, 108

Milky Way 26,
  29–31

moons 44, 48, 49,
  60, 61, 106

Mount Everest 79

Neptune 53,
  102–105, 108

North Star 18

Pistol Star 19

planets 50–53, 65,
  84, 93, 109

Pluto 35,
  106–107

Saturn 92–97,
  99, 108

solar eclipse
  45, 47

solar flares 37

solar system
  28, 74

stars 3, 8, 9,
  12–22, 24, 27,
  30, 31, 59

Sun 14, 17, 31,
  32–43, 52, 57,
  58, 101

supernovas 24–26

universe 2–5, 20
  74, 75

Uranus 98–101,
  108

Venus 55,
  62–69, 108

Raintree is an imprint of Capstone Global Library Limited, a company incorporated in England and Wales having its registered office at 7 Pilgrim Street, London, EC4V 6LB – Registered company number: 6695582

www.raintree.co.uk
myorders@raintree.co.uk

Edited by Shelly Lyons
Designed by Aruna Rangarajan
Photo Researcher: Svetlana Zhurkin
Creative Director: Nathan Gassman
Production by Lori Barbeau

ISBN 978 1 4747 0589 9
19 18 17 16 15
10 9 8 7 6 5 4 3 2 1

British Library Cataloguing in Publication Data
A full catalogue record for this book is available from the British Library.

Printed in China.

Acknowledgements
European Space Agency: DLR/FU Berlin, G. Neukum, 82—83, Planck Collaboration, 7; iStockphoto: PeopleImages, cover (bottom left), 8 (bottom); National Aeronautics and Space Administration: CXC/M. Weiss, 22, ESA/HEIC/The Hubble Heritage Team (STScI/AURA), cover (middle left), 8 (top), ESA/The Hubble Heritage Team (STScI/AURA), 10, ESA/J. Hester and A. Loll (Arizona State University), 24, Johns Hopkins University Applied Physics Laboratory/Carnegie Institution of Washington, 56—57, 60—61, JPL, 90—91, JPL/Space Science Institute, 85, 92—93, MOLA Science Team/O. de Goursac, Adrian Lark, 78—79, N. Walborn and J. Maíz-Apellániz (Space Telescope Science Institute, Baltimore, MD)/R. Barbá (La Plata Observatory, La Plata, Argentina), 13; Newscom: Design Pics/Carson Ganci, 14—15; Shutterstock: alexokokok, cover (top right), Alhovik, 106 (back), Ammit Jack, 49, Andrea Danti, 73, argus, 55, A-R-T, 48 (scroll), Asif Islam, 80, AstroStar, 26—27, bekulnis, 68, billdayone, 103, Byron W. Moore, 107, Christopher Ewing, 72, Christopher Gardiner, 18, Christos Georghiou, 34, Computer Earth, 35, Cory Thoman, 12 (right), 95 (right), Designsstock, 32—33, Fred Fokkelman, 50—51, Giantrabbit, 9, Givaga, 100, gnoparus, 28, gudinny, 94 (left), Gyvafoto, (right), Harvepino, 29, HelenField, 64—65, HuHu, 1, Igor Zh., 4, 5 (right), irin-k, 38 (left), ivn3da, 104, KMW Photography, 21 (bottom), kukaruka, 67, La Gorda, 95 (bubbles), lassedesignen, 77, Marcel Clemens, 101, Marija Piliponyte, 86, Mateusz Gzik, 74, Matthias Pahl, 66 (front), mayakova, 38 (right), Mega Pixel, 89 (bottom), Melica, 23, Memo Angeles, 12 (left), Michelangelus, 39, Milena Vuckovic, 54, Mopic, 58, Nadezda Razvodovska, 66 (back), Naeblys, 108—109, newyear, 59, Nikita Maykov, 30—31, NikoNomad, 76, Olga Danylenko, 5 (left), Orla, 52—53, owncham, 105, Pal Teravagimov, 79 (inset), Patrick Foto, 16, Pavel Smilyk, 3, Pixel Embargo, 97, R G Meier, 44, Rob Byro, 71, Sabphoto, back cover, 17, 42, Sebastian Crocker, 89 (top), SelenaMay, 62, SergeyDV, 96, TashaNatasha, 21 (back), Triff, cover (bottom right), 43, Tristan3D, 63, Vadim Sadovski, cover (top left), 102, ValoValo, 98, Vasilis Ververidis, 20, veronchick84, 94 (right), Vladimir Wrangel, 46, Voraorn Ratanakorn, 106 (top); SOHO (ESA & NASA), 37; SuperStock: Science and Society, 48 (front); Svetlana Zhurkin, 36; Wikimedia: Mike Young, 99

Design Elements by Capstone and Shutterstock